Helping Children See Jesus

ISBN: 978-1-933206-73-8

THE GRACE OF GOD
Old Testament Volume 19
Ruth

Author: Arlene S. Piepgrass
Illustrator: Vernon Henkel
Computer Graphic Artist: Yuko Kishimoto Willoughby
Typesetting and Layout: Morgan Melton, Patricia Pope

© 2018 Bible Visuals International
PO Box 153, Akron, PA 17501-0153
Phone: (717) 859-1131
www.biblevisuals.org

All rights reserved. No part of this publication may be reproduced, stored in a retrieval system or transmitted in any form by any means, electronic, mechanical, photocopy, recording or otherwise, without the prior permission of the publisher, except as provided by USA copyright law.

RELATED ITEMS

To access related items (such as activities, memory verse posters and translated texts) please visit our web store at shop.biblevisuals.org and enter 2019 in the search box on the page.

FREE TEXT DOWNLOAD

To access a FREE printable copy of the teaching text (PDF format) in English or other available languages, enter S2019DL in the search box. Add the item to your cart, and use coupon code XTACSV17 at checkout. Once your order is processed you will receive an email with a link to the free download.

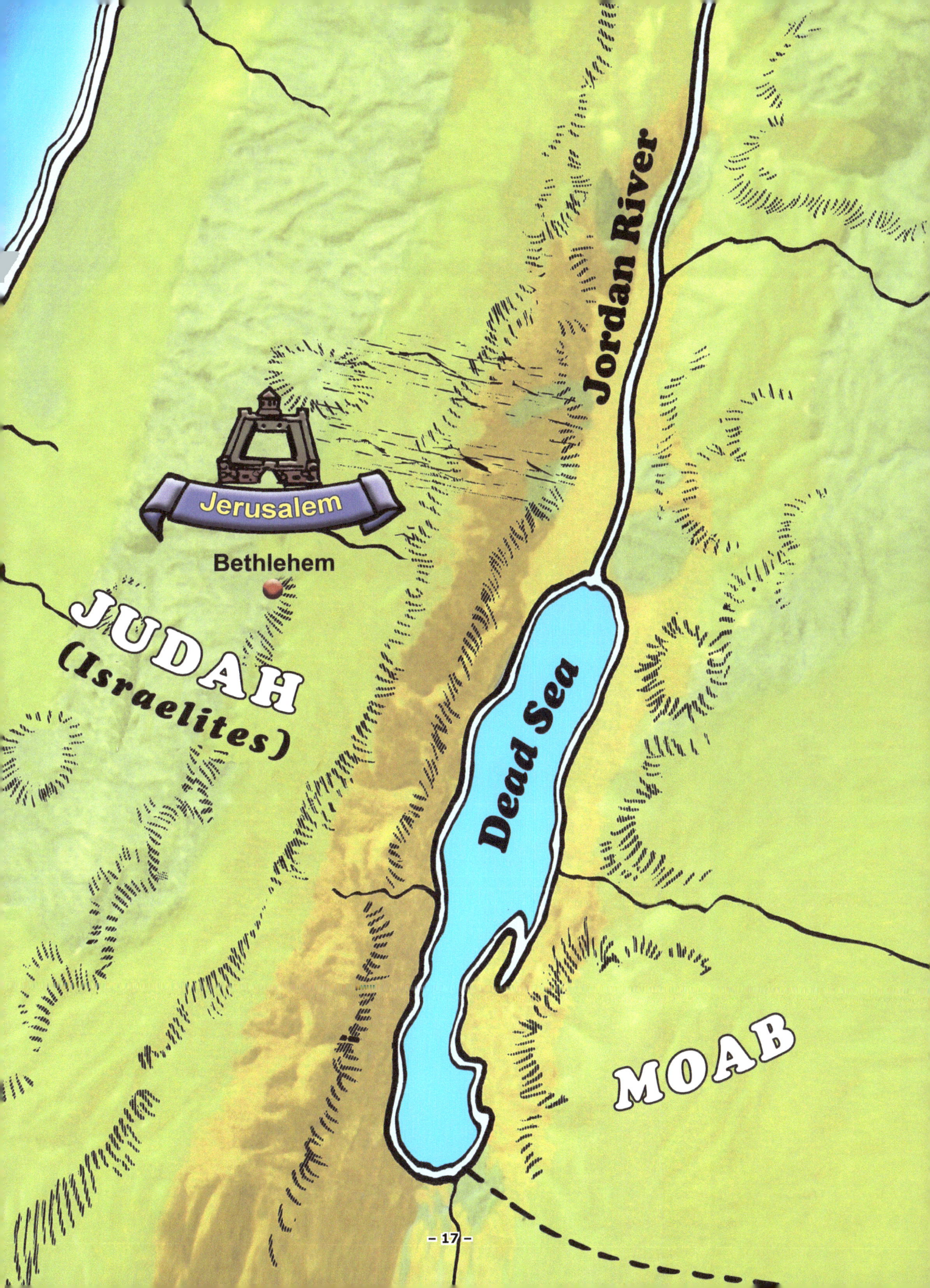

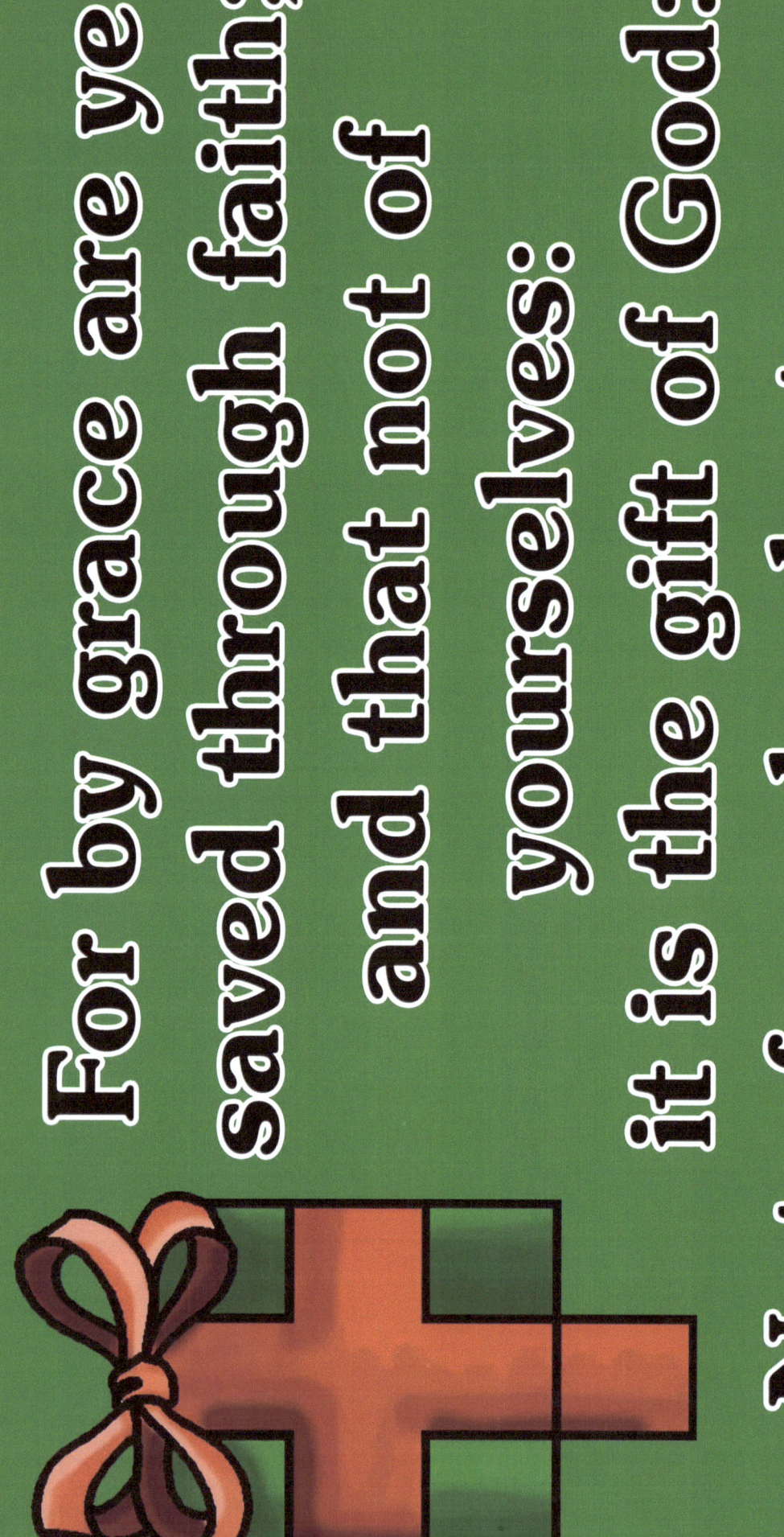

For by grace are ye saved through faith; and that not of yourselves: it is the gift of God: Not of works, lest any man should boast. Ephesians 2:8, 9

Lesson 1
GOD'S GRACE–SALVATION

NOTE TO THE TEACHER

Ruth is the record of a godly family living in the terrible times of the judges of Israel. During those years, "every man did that which was right in his own eyes" (Judges 17:6; 21:25).

In such a sin-filled setting, Ruth is a bright illustration of the grace of God and His abounding mercy.

Grace is God's provision for man's need. It is His eternal and absolutely free favor, shown in salvation which He offers to all.

The entire book of Ruth reveals the character and ways of God: His providence, sovereignty, grace, holiness, and His invitation of salvation to all people.

We do not deserve *anything* from God. He does not have to save us. Nor must He listen to us when we pray. He does not need to guide our lives, nor provide for our daily needs. But He does all this for us–and much, much more–because He is gracious.

One purpose of the book of Ruth is to show that even in the Old Testament the grace of God included the Gentiles.

Suggestions:

1. Have your students learn the song "Amazing Grace" at the time these lessons are taught.

2. If at all possible, use the *Ryrie Study Bible** with its excellent notes on the book of Ruth. All the notations throughout this particular edition of the Bible are extremely helpful.

3. If you have the book, *The Grace of God** by Dr. Charles C. Ryrie, study the Old Testament portions before you begin to teach the lessons on Ruth.

4. Print the following on a large piece of cardboard to be shown to class:

    GRACE = Undeserved Favor

    Display this sign whenever the subject of grace is mentioned.

    Because of God's grace, believers in Christ receive what we *do not* deserve–salvation; we *do not* receive what we *do* deserve–punishment for sin.

5. To illustrate the meaning of grace, use the opening story. Substitute for mayor the title of a local official known to your students.

* Available from Moody Press, Chicago, IL, 60610, U.S.A.

Scripture to be studied: Judges 3:12-30; Ruth 1:1-18; verses cited in lesson.

The *aim* of the lesson: In sovereign grace God calls people to trust in Him.

  What your students should *know*: God saves and blesses undeserving people.

  What your students should *feel*: Joyful because God–in His grace–saves even unworthy, sinful people.

  What your unsaved students should *do*: Receive salvation–the gift of God's grace.

Lesson outline for the teacher's and students' notebooks:

1. Ruth's childhood (Judges 3:12-30).
2. Ruth meets Elimelech's family (Ruth 1:1-2).
3. Ruth influenced by Naomi (Ruth 1:3-5).
4. Ruth's decision (Ruth 1:6-18).

The verses to be memorized:

> *For by grace are ye saved through faith; and that not of yourselves: it is the gift of God: Not of works, lest any man should boast.* (Ephesians 2:8-9)

(*Teacher:* Use Ephesians 2:4-10 for more advanced students.)

THE LESSON

One day the mayor of a large city commanded an officer: "Go to the poorest section of our city and bring six of the neediest children to my home."

When the boys and girls stood before the mayor, they were terrified. Imagine their surprise, therefore, when he said, "I'm going to adopt you. I will provide you with food, clothing, schooling, and everything you need. From now on, you are my children."

What did these six do to deserve such goodness from the mayor? (*Nothing!*) Did they pay for this favor? Did they work for it? Did the mayor have to be kind to them? NO! Only because of his grace did he provide for these children. All they had to do was receive his gifts.

Today we begin a study of the little Bible book entitled *Ruth*. In our lessons on Ruth we will learn about the *Grace of God*–His undeserved favor. No one is entitled to His goodness. No one is worthy of His love. We can do nothing to earn God's kindness. It is not necessary for God to do anything for anyone. But because of His marvelous grace, He provides salvation and everything that is good for everyone.

1. RUTH'S CHILDHOOD
Judges 3:12-30

Ruth was born in the land of Moab. (Indicate on back cover map.) Moab was near the land of Israel. But the Moabites and Israelites were enemies. Years before, God cursed the Moabites because they had been unfriendly to the people of Israel (when they were on their way from Egypt to Canaan–Deuteronomy 23:3-4).

Show Illustration #1

In Moab, Ruth's parents taught her about their gods–particularly the one called Chemosh. (See Numbers 21:29.) Ruth was horrified whenever she looked at this ugly idol. She knew that many human sacrifices had been offered to it. (See 2 Kings 3:26-27.) This filled her with terror.

According to the Jewish book called the *Midrash*, Ruth was the daughter of Eglon. He was the very fat king of Moab. (See Judges 3:17.)

God allowed King Eglon to conquer the Israelites because they had turned from worshiping Him. Quickly the rebellious people of Israel learned the awfulness of being ruled by a cruel king (Judges 3:12-30).

– 19 –

Ruth probably heard her father speak often about the Israelites. "They say our idol, Chemosh, is a false god. They believe their God is the only God," he would say with a smirk on his face. "They even call themselves 'the people of the living God.' Well, they might be the people God has chosen for Himself. But they are our slaves! They ought to know by now that their God cannot protect them from us."

So for 18 years the Moabites had ruled over the people of Israel. But when the Israelites truly repented of their rebellion and turned to God again, He forgave them. Then He helped a young Israelite man named Ehud to kill King Eglon of Moab. At last the people of Israel were free from the power of the Moabites.

2. RUTH MEETS ELIMELECH'S FAMILY
Ruth 1:1-2

Some time later, news spread through the Moabite countryside where Ruth lived: "A new family has moved into our village. They are Israelites from Bethlehem and have two sons!"

All the girls were eager to meet these strangers–especially the two sons, named Mahlon and Chilion.

As the months went by, Ruth and Mahlon became interested in each other. And Chilion liked Ruth's friend, Orpah.

Show Illustration #2

Of course Mahlon and Chilion invited Ruth and Orpah to their home to meet their parents. We do not know exactly what the girls said, but it could have been something like this . . .

"Why did you leave your home in Bethlehem to come down here to Moab?" Ruth asked.

Elimelech, the father of the young men, answered sadly, "A severe famine ruined us. We didn't have enough food. Our God had given that area to us (Deuteronomy 1:8), we didn't want to leave. But I felt as if I had no choice. I thought my family and I would starve to death."

"Couldn't your God take care of your needs?" asked Orpah.

Neither Elimelech nor Naomi, his wife, answered. They knew God had sent the famine to discipline His rebellious, idol-worshiping people.

3. RUTH INFLUENCED BY NAOMI
Ruth 1:3-5

The girls continued visiting the home of the four from Bethlehem. Ruth especially enjoyed talking to Naomi. "Tell me more about your God," she often said.

"Many years ago the Lord God led our people out of Egypt. There they had been slaves for over 400 years," Naomi explained. "Traveling through the wild, barren land between Egypt and Canaan was extremely hard. Our people, the Israelites, often disobeyed God. And they complained continually. Nevertheless the Lord loved them. Every day He gave them food to eat. He taught them how to worship Him. He often spoke to their leader, Moses.

"Forty years later, the Lord led our people into Canaan–the fertile land He had promised to give them. (See Joshua 5:6.) Beforehand God promised to care for them. He agreed to supply all their needs if they would obey Him and worship Him alone. *BUT* He also warned our people that there would be a famine if they disobeyed Him and worshiped the idols and false gods of the people in Canaan." (See Leviticus 26:1, 14-20; Deuteronomy 11:16-17.)

With tears in her eyes, Naomi added, "Most of our people forgot the true and living God of Heaven–even rebelled against Him. Then they began to worship the gods of the Canaanites–idols which could not help them." (See Judges 2:10-11, 13.)

Naomi continued, "Our God means what He says. He kept His promises in those days long ago. And He carries out His promises and enforces His warnings today. He now has made the sky as brass. He has withheld the rain. There is no food for our people."

Ruth thought, *How different Naomi's God is from our ugly idol Chemosh! The God of Heaven speaks to His people. He warns them against disobedience. He keeps His promises. I would rather worship Him than offer sacrifices to Chemosh.*

Ruth was learning from Naomi about the true and living God–and what He is like. Ruth learned these truths–not because of her goodness, but because of God's GRACE. He loved her and wanted her to know about Himself. (*Teacher:* Display card and explain the meaning of *Grace*.)

Months passed. There was much happy laughter in that home. For Ruth and Mahlon, and Orpah and Chilion were discussing with Naomi and Elimelech their plans for marriage. Suddenly, before the wedding day, Elimelech died. From then on the home was filled with sadness.

Ruth watched Naomi in her sorrow. She did not wail as Orpah and the people of Moab did. Nor did she try to please God by offering sacrifices as the Moabites did. Naomi was sad. But because she prayed often to the true and living God, He comforted her.

In time, the two young couples were married. They were kind to Naomi and cared for her. But another sadness came to that household: Neither Mahlon and Ruth nor Chilion and Orpah had any children.

Show Illustration #3

In addition, Mahlon and Chilion were often sick. It was hard for them to care for the growing crops. Day after day they became weaker. Finally both died.

Naomi was greatly troubled. She loved her daughters-in-law, Ruth and Orpah. But they were Moabites. She missed her own people, the Israelites. She longed to worship the Lord God in her homeland.

4. RUTH'S DECISION
Ruth 1:16-18

Naomi looked sadder each day. She spent hours sitting by her window gazing toward Bethlehem.

One day Ruth said to Naomi, "You are not happy here, are you?"

"My God has allowed me to have very sad experiences," Naomi complained.

We might have reminded her: "Naomi, you and your husband left the land which the Lord gave you and your people. Instead of trusting Him, you decided to go to a pagan land to make a better living. Now you are suffering because of your *own* decision."

How much easier it is to blame the Lord than to admit our own sinful mistakes!

One day an Israelite traveler passing through brought good news. "Naomi, you should see your home town, Bethlehem!" he said. "There is plenty of food for everyone. The fields are producing a rich harvest. Our God has heard our prayers. He has once again blessed our land."

Naomi's eyes shone. "I am going home," she declared firmly. "That is where I belong. The people of Moab are not my people. The gods of Moab are not my gods. My God–the true and living God of Heaven–has not forgotten me. He will go before me and help me."

Naomi began to pack her few belongings for the return trip to Bethlehem.

"I'm going with you," Ruth announced.

"So am I," Orpah echoed.

Early in the morning the three women left their small home and started down the mountain toward the Jordan River. (Indicate on back cover map.) At the river Naomi stopped to rest.

Turning to Ruth and Orpah, she said, "Go back now to your mothers' homes. There you will be cared for. You've been kind to me and I appreciate it. But you must return to Moab. Your friends are there. I trust you will soon have Moabite husbands."

With tears streaming down her face, Naomi hugged Ruth and Orpah.

"No, no, don't leave us!" the two begged, clinging to Naomi. "We want to go with you."

"Why?" asked Naomi. "You would be foreigners in my land."

Orpah thought for a few moments and decided not to go. Picking up her belongings, she hugged Naomi again and turned to climb the mountain to her home. We never again hear Orpah mentioned in the rest of the Bible.

Show Illustration #4

But Ruth clung to Naomi. Naomi spoke to her tenderly, "Why don't you go with Orpah? She's returning to her people–and her gods."

Ruth shivered at the thought of Chemosh. Long ago she had learned it was an ugly, helpless idol. Before Mahlon died, she had placed her trust in the living God of Heaven. Looking into Naomi's eyes, she firmly replied, "I am going with you!" (*Teacher:* Read Ruth's decision, Ruth 1:16-17.)

Together the two women stepped into a little boat and crossed the Jordan River. They were on their way to Bethlehem.

Ruth was no better than anyone else in Moab. The Moabite people chose to worship man-made false gods. But because of His grace, God the Lord helped Ruth choose to trust in Himself.

Let's think what the Lord did to cause Ruth to trust in Him:

1. God brought an Israelite family into Ruth's life.
2. The Israelite family told of worshiping the true God.
3. God gave Ruth understanding of the difference between the true God and Chemosh.
4. Finally Ruth decided to turn from her false gods to the living God.

Because of the grace of God, Orpah had the same opportunity to turn to Him. But she decided it was too hard to give up her family and her homeland. She was content to worship the idols of Moab. So she turned her back on the gracious One who offered her His love, His care, His comfort.

Today–because of His grace–God has talked to you about Himself. Do you understand God's love for you? Is it clear to you that because of His loving grace, He provided a Saviour for you? (Teacher: Briefly explain the significance of Christ's death and resurrection.)

Now, because you know this, you must decide whether or not you will receive God's Son. He was sent from Heaven by God the Father. When you place all your trust in the Son of God, asking Him to forgive your sin, you will be born into the family of God. The decision you make will change your life here on earth. And it will decide where you will spend eternity. (Encourage your students to make this decision right now.)

Lesson 2
GOD'S GRACE–PROVISION

NOTE TO THE TEACHER

Someone has written: "The book of Ruth is like a little window through which the light of God pours in to clarify truth seen elsewhere."

The truth of God's provision for His children is dramatized in this lesson. As Ruth yielded herself totally to the Lord, He graciously supplied her needs. She had not understood all that was involved when she turned to the true and living God, but she followed Him one step at a time. She believed He would care for her. And He did.

There are many promises in the Bible assuring us that the Lord will provide for us today. (See, for example: Proverbs 3:5-6; Philippians 4:19.) We don't deserve His care. But He gives it because of His loving favor. This is GRACE.

Plainly display the poster defining GRACE.

Review:

1. Salvation is something we do not deserve, nor can we work for it. It is a GIFT from God. We neither buy nor work for gifts which are given to us.
2. Discuss briefly the decisions which Ruth and Orpah made. Emphasize the results of their choices. Again remind students that each can decide to turn to the Lord and have His salvation and blessing. By turning from Him, they will spend eternity apart from Him.

Scriptured to be studied: Ruth 1:19–2:23

The *aim* of the lesson: Because of His grace, God provides for His own.

  What your students should *know*: God wants us to enjoy all He has planned for us.

  What your students should *feel*: Thanksgiving to God for supplying every need.

  What your students should *do*: Make a list of the Lord's provisions.

Lesson outline for the teacher's and students' notebooks:

1. God provides direction for Ruth (Ruth 1:19-2:3).
2. God provides acceptance for Ruth (Ruth 2:4-13).
3. God provides food and fellowship for Ruth (Ruth 2:14-17).
4. God provides joy for Naomi (Ruth 2:19-23).

The verses to be memorized:

For by grace are ye saved through faith; and that not of yourselves: it is the gift of God: Not of works, lest any man should boast. (Ephesians 2:8-9)

(*Teacher:* Use Ephesians 2:4-10 for more advanced students.)

THE LESSON

Let's pretend we're meeting Ruth and Naomi as they step as they step out of the little boat after crossing the Jordan River. (On map, indicate the Jordan River and Bethlehem.)

As we walk beside them, climbing the Judean hills toward Bethlehem, we have some questions.

"Naomi, what are you thinking about?" you ask.

How do you think she would answer? (Encourage student response.)

Naomi, walking slowly, replies sadly. "I was thinking about the day ten years ago when I walked down here with Elimelech, Mahlon, and Chilion. We were a happy family. But because of the famine here, we thought our lives would be better in Moab.

"Returning now, I've behind those who were dearest to me in graves in Moab. I'm going home empty."

A bit later–her voice sounding brighter–she added, "But I am thankful that God is letting me go back to my people."

Turning, you ask, "Ruth, what are you thinking about?"

How do you think she would answer? (Let students suggest her thoughts.)

"I am a little frightened," Ruth says quietly. "I have left everything I am used to–my family, my homeland, my friends. I left my gods, too," she adds firmly. "I hated those idols! How thankful I am that I heard of the living God! I want to learn more about Him. I want to worship Him!"

"How will you earn a living when you get to Bethlehem?" you ask Ruth.

"I don't know. My husband, Mahlon, is dead. I have no one here on earth to provide for me. But Naomi says God will take care of us. We are praying to Him, believing He will give us all we need," says Ruth confidently.

1. GOD PROVIDES DIRECTION FOR RUTH
Ruth 1:19-2:3

The two women finally arrived in Bethlehem. It seemed the whole town came out to greet them.

"Is this really Naomi?" the women whispered among themselves. "She looks old and sad."

Turning to Naomi, one asked, "Where is Elimelech? Did Mahlon and Chilion stay in Moab?"

"Life has been very bitter for me," answered Naomi. "We left as a happy family. Now my husband and sons are buried in Moab."

Naomi's old friends shook their heads sadly, sympathizing with her.

"But the Lord is good to bring me back to you," Naomi added, hugging one and another.

Naomi drew Ruth close to her. "I want you to meet my daughter-in-law, Ruth," she began. "She married Mahlon. Ever since Elimelech and my sons died, my daughters-in-law have taken loving care of me. Ruth, choosing to leave the gods of Moab, has turned to our true and living God of Heaven. And she wanted to come with me. I pray you will love and accept her."

Ruth and Naomi found a small house where they could stay. It didn't take them long to unpack their few belongings.

"This little bit of food we brought will soon be gone," Ruth began. She set her small sack of grain on the shelf. "As we walked today, I saw that the barley is being harvested. Could I go to one of the fields and gather the leftover grain? Do you think someone would show favor to me, a foreigner?"

"Oh, yes!" replied Naomi quickly. "In His laws, our God has made special provision for foreigners and widows like you and me." (Read Leviticus 19:1, 10; Deuteronomy 24:19. Let students discuss the Lord's gracious provision mentioned in these verses.)

So early the next morning, Ruth put on her working clothes. She wondered, *Where should I begin searching for a field in which to gather grain*? But what do you suppose she and Naomi would have done before she left? (Let students respond.)

Show Illustration #5

I believe they prayed and asked the Lord to guide Ruth to the best field.

(*Teacher:* Read aloud Ruth 2:3.) Boaz was a wealthy, godly man. Do you think Ruth simply "happened" to choose his field? (Encourage discussion.) No, indeed! God directed her there. Ruth didn't know yet that this was so. But the Lord was working out a wonderful plan for her life.

2. GOD PROVIDES ACCEPTANCE FOR RUTH
Ruth 2:4-13

It was almost lunch time when Ruth saw a distinguished looking man in the field. She thought, *Can he be the owner of this land*? She saw him move among the workers, greeting them kindly.

Watching from the corner of her eye, she saw him pointing at her as he talked to the man in charge. Now he was walking toward her. *Will he tell me not to gather grain in his field*? she wondered fearfully.

Show Illustration #6

Listen to what Boaz said to Ruth. (Print Ruth 2:8 on chalkboard and read. Discuss his generosity and kindness.)

How do you think Ruth felt when she heard this? What would you have done if Boaz had said these kind words to you? (Allow discussion.)

Ruth was overwhelmed. The Bible says she bowed down with her face to the ground asking, "Why are you so kind to me? Do you not know that I am a foreigner?"

"Yes, I know all about you," Boaz answered quietly. How do you think he knew about Ruth? (News travels quickly in a small town.) What do you think he had heard about her? (Discuss, then read Ruth 2:11.)

"You have chosen to trust in the Lord God," said Boaz. "I pray He will bless you."

I wonder if Boaz thought of his own mother, Rahab (spelled Rachab in Matthew 1:5), when he met Ruth. (Review briefly the account of Rahab, Joshua 2. She, too, turned from the false gods of her people in Canaan. She chose, instead, to leave her people and serve the true and living God of Heaven.)

"Oh, thank you, sir," Ruth replied humbly. "You are surely kind and I am not even one of your workers. I hope I shall continue to find favor in your eyes."

Yes, Boaz was showing favor–grace–to Ruth. She did not deserve to be considered as one of his workers. But he accepted her and allowed her to pick up left-over grain in his fields. He was also accepting her as an Israelite, asking the Lord's blessing on her.

The true and living God whom Ruth had chosen to trust was providing for her far more than she ever expected. (See Ephesians 3:20.)

3. GOD PROVIDES FOOD AND FELLOWSHIP FOR RUTH
Ruth 2:14-17

"It's time to eat!" called the man in charge.

The reapers stopped working and gathered in the shade with Boaz. Ruth sat alone in a spot where she would not be seen.

But someone did see her. "Come eat with us," Boaz called.

Show Illustration #7

Making space for her, he also made sure she had enough food.

I am only a poor foreigner. Yet Boaz is wonderfully kind to me, Ruth thought to herself. *He has made this an easy day for me. He has provided much more than I ever expected.*

When Ruth went back to gather left-over grain, Boaz warned his workers: "I do not want you men to bother that young woman. Do not embarrass her in any way. While you are harvesting, drop some of the grain on purpose so it will be easy for her to gather what she needs."

Turning to the women reapers, he said, "I want you to be friendly to Ruth. She is a foreigner. She needs your kindness and understanding."

Why do you think Boaz was kind to Ruth? (Let students discuss.) As a godly man, he would show grace–the grace of God. This is what the Lord wants to see in each of His children. Do you think Boaz had anything else in mind?

4. GOD PROVIDES JOY FOR NAOMI
Ruth 2:19-23

What do you suppose Naomi–at home–was thinking about all day? (Have students respond.) I believe her thoughts were something like this: *I wonder if Ruth found a good field in which to pick up grain. Were the reapers kind to her? Did she find enough grain?*

Naomi could hardly wait until evening when Ruth would return. When she saw her coming, Naomi ran to meet her.

Show Illustration #8

"Oh, you gathered so much!" she rejoiced. "Where did you work? Someone has surely been kind to you. I pray that the Lord will bless that man."

"I worked in the field of Boaz," Ruth answered. "He was so very thoughtful. He even told me to stay in his fields during the entire barley season."

"In the field of Boaz!" Naomi exclaimed. "He is one of our close relatives! God has heard our prayers and led you there today. The Lord has not forgotten us! He is showing His kindness to our family."

For the first time in months, Naomi's face shone with joy. Many times in the past years she was afraid God had forgotten her. Sometimes she felt He was punishing her. Now she knew that the Lord is faithful. He does care for His children.

Ruth had committed her life to God. She did not know how He would care for her. But she trusted Him. And He led her, blessed her, and provided for her in ways she herself could never have arranged.

Would you like to have the Lord provide for you as He did for Ruth? He will if you have truly placed your trust in His Son, the Lord Jesus Christ.

1. God promises to *accept you* if you trust the Lord Jesus as your Saviour (Ephesians 1:6-7).
2. God promises to *direct you* if you acknowledge Him (Proverbs 3:5-6).
3. God promises to *provide* all you need (Philippians 4:19).
4. God promises *joy* if you yield yourself to Him (John 15:11).

He doesn't provide these blessings because His own people deserve them. He gives them because of His *grace*.

During this week make a list of what the Lord provides for you. Bring it to class to share with us in our next session.

(Before dismissing class, have students sing, "Count Your Many Blessings".)

Lesson 3
GOD'S GRACE—PROTECTION

NOTE TO THE TEACHER

God had a wonderful plan for Ruth's life. His plan was far better than anything she had ever hoped for. Ruth didn't know it, but *in His grace* the Lord God chose her as an ancestor of His Son, the Saviour, Jesus Christ. God worked in the lives of various people to accomplish this purpose.

As the lesson unfolds, we see the Lord protecting Ruth in her daily life. She submitted herself to Him and to her elders because of their relationship to God.

In the fourth point of the lesson, Ruth's action was in accord with the law which required the initiative of the widow to seek the marriage. (See Deuteronomy 25:5, 7-10.) Ruth, by her actions, indicated "her desire to have Boaz, who had given every evidence of willingness to perform the duties of kinsman redeemer." (From note in *Ryrie Study Bible*, page 406.)

The Lord has chosen each of us "to be conformed to the image of His Son" (Romans 8:29) and to glorify Him (1 Corinthians 6:20). When we try to direct our own lives instead of allowing God to plan our lives, there is disaster and heartache. In this lesson, continually remind your students of Proverbs 3:5-6. Ruth acknowledged the Lord and He directed and protected her far beyond anything she could ask or think.

Review the highlights of the previous chapter before beginning today's lesson. Have students read or tell what the Lord provided for them during the past week.

If possible, to introduce this lesson take two flowers to class. One must be a bud, the other a flower already opened. In class, force the bud open. Then compare it to the flower which opened naturally as God designed. This one will be beautiful, the other ruined, because of unnatural force. Explain that this is an example of our lives. The heavenly Father has a perfect plan. He will protect us and provide everything which is needed to accomplish His plan. But when we interfere and insist on going our own way, our lives–like the bud–are spoiled.

Scripture to be studied: Ruth 1:1-2; 2:21-23; 3:1-18

The *aim* of the lesson: God works out His purpose in the lives of His own.

What your students should *know*: Things do not "happen"; everything is controlled by God.

What your students should *feel*: Awe, because of God's control in even the smallest details of a person's life.

What your students should *do*: Yield their lives to God for His use.

Lesson outline for the teacher's and students' notebooks:

1. Naomi tried to protect her family (Ruth 1:1-2).
2. God's protection (Ruth 2:21-23).
3. Protection provided in God's law (Deuteronomy 25:5-10; Leviticus 25:48).
4. God protects the family line of His anointed Son–the Messiah (Ruth 3:1-18).

The verse to be memorized:

For by grace are ye saved through faith; and that not of yourselves: it is the gift of God: Not of works, lest any man should boast. (Ephesians 2:8-9)

(Use Ephesians 2:4-10 for more advanced students.)

THE LESSON

1. NAOMI TRIED TO PROTECT HER FAMILY
Ruth 1:1-2

Ruth and Naomi enjoyed their evening meal. I wonder if their conversation went something like this:

Naomi exclaimed, "Ruth, our God is indeed gracious! I do not deserve the kindness He has shown to you and me today."

Then she began to talk of the past. "Your father-in-law, Elimelech, and I never should have left Bethlehem. The Lord promised to care for us always here in this land where He had placed us. When conditions became difficult and food scarce, we thought we could protect our sons from suffering by going to Moab. Elimelech and I didn't pray for God's guidance. We made our own decisions."

Show Illustration #9

She continued, "Moab wasn't the Lord's place for us. We selected that area ourselves. We chose to go there because of our fear of hunger. We didn't trust God. Our plans ended in death and sorrow. If only we had let our heavenly Father provide for our family, everything would be different today!"

If only are two sad words. Many people today are saying, "If only . . ." Why? Because they chose their own way rather than God's way for their lives.

Ruth listened as Naomi spoke with hope in her voice. "I am old, Ruth. I will not have another son for you to marry. But I know now that the Lord has not forgotten us."

2. GOD'S PROTECTION
Ruth 2:21-23

Naomi asked, "Did you say Boaz invited you back to his field tomorrow?"

"Yes, he told me to stay close to his girl reapers," answered Ruth.

Naomi knew there were many young men in the harvest fields who might harm Ruth. Ruth was a foreigner. She was beautiful and young. These were the days of the judges when every man did as he pleased. (See Judges 17:6; 21:25.) Immoral sin and idolatry were practiced. Naomi saw the dangers. She didn't want Ruth to be abused in any way.

Show Illustration #10

Therefore Naomi warned Ruth saying, "Don't go to any other field. Keep away from the young men. Stay with the girls in the field of Boaz."

Ruth could have thought, *I shall do as I please. Naomi is an old woman. She does not want me to have any fun. Why*

– 24 –

should she tell me to stay away from those young men?

But Ruth had no such thoughts. Instead, she was probably thinking, *Naomi loves me. I know she wants the best for me. She has worshiped the true God longer than I have. I will listen to what she says.*

Are you like Ruth? Your parents have warned you against becoming friendly with those who have bad habits. They know these people could harm you. Do you obey your parents? Or do you do as you please with no respect for your parents?

(*Teacher:* Emphasize that:

1. Obedience to parents is a command of God. (See Exodus 20:12; Ephesians 6:1; Colossians 3:20.)
2. Parents desire the best for their children even though it may not seem so.)

The days and weeks went by quickly and happily for Ruth. She made friends of the other girls in the field. Gathering enough grain was easy because Boaz had told the reapers to drop some grain on purpose for her.

Ruth loved the beauty of Bethlehem. She loved the friendliness of the people. The sadness was gone from her eyes. Naomi often heard her sing and laugh.

Ruth especially loved her mother-in-law. Each evening they talked together about the happenings of the day. Naomi observed that Ruth often mentioned Boaz. It seemed that having lunch with him and his workers was the highlight of her day.

"He is a fine man," Ruth told Naomi. "Every day when he comes to work he greets us saying, 'The Lord be with you!' And the workers always answer, 'The Lord bless you!' We all respect him and he is kind to everyone."

It was not hard for Naomi to see that Ruth loved Boaz. Nightly, after Ruth went to bed, Naomi sat thinking.

3. PROTECTION PROVIDED IN GOD'S LAW
Deuteronomy 25:5-10; Leviticus 25:48

Two matters were extremely important to every Israelite family:

1. That the land which God had given them be kept in the family.
2. That a son and grandsons would carry on the family name.

Show Illustration #11

Naomi now owned the land which had belonged to Elimelech. But she no longer had a son to whom to give it. And there were no grandsons to carry on the family name.

The Lord God had given a law to the Israelites to protect women like Naomi. And Naomi knew God's laws well.

She thought to herself, *The Lord has commanded concerning a widow who has no son, that the nearest relative must marry her*. (See Deuteronomy 25:5-10; Leviticus 25:48. The first son born of such a marriage would continue the original family name, and would inherit the family property.) *Boaz is a close relative. Though he is older than Ruth, he seems to be attracted to her. And it is easy to see that she loves him. I wonder if he would be willing to buy my land. If he would, then he could marry Ruth. He would make her extremely happy. And if they would have a son, Elimelech's name would continue!* Naomi bowed her head and thanked the Lord for remembering her family. He had provided abundantly for them during the harvest season. Now it seemed He might protect her family name and property! So, with God's Law in mind, she decided on a plan.

4. GOD PROTECTS THE FAMILY LINE OF HIS ANOINTED SON —THE MESSIAH
Ruth 3:1-18

The next morning Ruth listened as Naomi unfolded her plan–God's plan. It was entirely different from the customs of the Moabites.

What will Boaz think of me? she wondered as Naomi explained what she should do.

Surely Naomi wouldn't ask me to do anything wrong. Since this is God's Law, I'll do what she says. Her God is my God. He will continue to protect me just as He has these past months, thought Ruth.

Instead of going for grain, Ruth worked at home. She followed Naomi's instructions perfectly–preparing for the evening. One minute Ruth was singing happily. But the next minute she was doubtful and frightened.

Before sundown, she put on her best clothes and a long wrap to keep her warm in the night air. Standing before Naomi she asked, "How do I look?"

"You're beautiful, Ruth," Naomi murmured softly. "Don't be afraid. The Lord will protect you. What you are going to do is commanded by Him in His Law." (See Deuteronomy 25:5-10.)

At sunset, Ruth stepped out onto the village street. What a festive spirit was felt in the little town! Everyone was singing happily. There was great rejoicing for the abundant harvest after weeks of hard work. Ruth listened to their songs which told of the goodness of the Lord to them. How different from harvest time in Moab! There they burned incense to the ugly idols they brought out of the dark temples. Here they sang to the Lord God in whom they trusted. How glad she was that she, too, knew the true and living God of Heaven!

Ruth mingled with the crowd as they made their way to the threshing floor outside the village. (*Teacher:* Explain that this was a large open area where the grain was beaten to separate it from the chaff.) Ruth stood in the shadows watching families sit down to eat. Afterward the children, young people, and women– all but Ruth–returned to their homes. The men prepared to sleep on the threshing floor beside their piles of grain. They feared that their enemies, the Midianites, might come in the night to steal the grain if they didn't guard it. (See Judges 6:1-6.)

Ruth remembered Naomi's instructions. From a hiding place, she saw Boaz lie down. Without moving even a finger, she waited until everyone was asleep. Then she tiptoed to the place where Boaz was sleeping. Exactly as Naomi had told her to do, she lifted his flowing robe uncovering his feet. Silently she lay at his feet, her heart pounding wildly. (*Teacher:* Doesn't this remind you of being protected under the "wings of the Almighty"? Psalm 91:1, 4.)

Will Boaz be angry when he finds me here? Ruth wondered. "Dear Lord, please protect me and help me," she prayed. And she waited.

In the middle of the night, Boaz realized someone was at his feet. *Can it be a thief?* he wondered. "Who's there?" he demanded.

Show Illustration #12

"I am your servant, Ruth," she whispered. "My mother-in-law, Naomi, told me that, according to God's Law, I should ask if I may be your wife. You are a close relative, you know."

Her heart thumped faster. *What will he say? Will he refuse to marry me?*

What do you think Boaz said? (Let students respond. Read Ruth 3:10-11 slowly. Emphasize the good testimony Ruth had. She was a foreigner and a widow. Her excellent conduct won for her a good reputation in Bethlehem.)

"I love you, Ruth," Boaz whispered. "And I should be happy to buy Naomi's land and marry you. However, we have a problem. Another man is a closer relative than I. If he wants to redeem you, I must let him. If not, I shall redeem you." (*Teacher:* Explain that "to redeem" meant *to buy back* the land and marry the widow.)

"I will talk to the closer relative in the morning," Boaz promised.

Taking her shawl, Boaz poured grain on it, and tied it. "Here is a gift for Naomi," he said.

At home, Naomi could scarcely wait for Ruth to return. When she did arrive and explained all that had taken place, Naomi was overjoyed.

"Just wait, Ruth," Naomi said. "Boaz will settle the matter today!"

Did Boaz marry Ruth? Or did the closer relative marry her?

"Just wait!" That is what Naomi said. "WAIT!" But waiting is hard! Let me tell you this: Someone much greater than Naomi had planned Ruth's life. And He had a more wonderful purpose for Ruth's life than she, Naomi, or Boaz could possibly dream.

Even before He created the world, God planned to send His Son, the Lord Jesus Christ, into the world to die for sinners. And He planned that Christ Jesus would be born into the earthly family of David, who became king of Israel. Let me tell you something marvelous which Ruth did not know: The Lord had chosen her to be the great grandmother of King David! How wonderful is His *grace*!

God was able to work out His gracious purpose in Ruth's life because she yielded her life totally to Him. She refused to make plans of her own. Instead, she allowed the Lord to choose for her.

Would you like to follow God's plan for your life? He will guard your life for His purpose if you let Him. Right now, will you bow your head and tell the Lord you want to follow His plan for your life?

(*Teacher:* Encourage any who respond to remain after class. Explain to them that the Lord uses parents, teachers, and preachers to guide them in their conduct and decisions. Studying the Bible enables them to know what God wants them to do. If they follow His will today, tomorrow, and each day, they will be in His will in the years ahead.)

Lesson 4
GOD'S GRACE—REDEMPTION

NOTE TO THE TEACHER

In this lesson you will use the Biblical expressions *Redeem* and *Redeemer*. To help your students understand these words and their meanings, print them on large cards for display.

Redeem: to set free by paying a price (ransom).

Redeemer: the person who pays the ransom price.

The introduction to the book of Ruth in the *Ryrie Study Bible* gives this splendid help:

Boaz, the kinsman-redeemer, serves as a beautiful type of Christ, in that:

1. He was a blood relative (Romans 1:3; Hebrews 2:14);
2. He had the price with which to purchase the forfeited inheritance (1 Peter 1:18-19);
3. He was willing to redeem (Hebrews 10:7).

Throughout this lesson emphasize our need for a heavenly Redeemer and Christ's willingness and power to redeem us. Because He–the eternal One–became a human, He is our Kinsman: our Kinsman-Redeemer.

Before teaching the lesson, display the sign: *Grace = Undeserved favor*. Discuss the three previous lessons mentioning God's favor shown to Ruth in: salvation, provision, and protection. From eternity past, God had silently, lovingly planned for her.

David lived 3000 years ago: Ruth and Boaz, three generations before him. These events which God recorded in His Word, help us to understand His love and redemption. Be certain your students perfectly understand the meanings of *Redeem* and *Redeemer*. If these expressions are not entirely clear, the lesson will not be understood.

Scripture to be studied: Ruth 4; verses cited in lesson.

The *aim* of the lesson: To explain the meaning of redemption.

What your students should *know*: Christ came to earth to redeem sinful people.

What your students should *feel*: A desire to become a member of the family of God.

What your students should *do*:
Saved: Yield their lives to the Lord.
Unsaved: Believe on the Lord Jesus Christ so they can become members of the family of God.

Lesson outline for the teacher's and students' notebooks:

1. Desire of Boaz to redeem Ruth (Ruth 4:1-4).
2. The natural unworthiness of Ruth (Ruth 4:5-6).
3. Boaz redeems Ruth (Ruth 4:7-12).
4. The blessings of redemption (Ruth 4:13-17).

The verses to be memorized:

For by grace are ye saved through faith; and that not of yourselves: it is the gift of God: Not of works, lest any man should boast. (Ephesians 2:8-9)

(*Teacher:* Ephesians 2:4-10 for more advanced students.)

THE LESSON

1. DESIRE OF BOAZ TO REDEEM RUTH
Ruth 4:1-4

After reviewing the previous lessons, say to the class: "As we study about Ruth and Boaz today, I want you to think how Ruth reminds you of yourself. Think about how Boaz was like our Lord Jesus Christ."

As soon as the sun came up, Boaz left the threshing floor. Quickly he made his way to the village. Already the streets were buzzing with activity. Donkeys, weighed down with heavy loads, crowded through the city gates. Women, balancing empty water pots on their heads, made their way to the well.

At the market place noisy buyers and sellers bargained about prices of foods and wares. Wealthy farmers and merchants mingled among the peasants, beggars, blind and crippled.

Boaz hurried to the Bethlehem gate. It was in this place that important business was conducted. He scanned the crowd searching for one person. For whom was he looking? (*The closest relative of Naomi.*) Why was he eager to find him? (*Boaz hoped the closest relative would not be able to redeem Ruth. Boaz loved her and wanted to redeem her for himself.*)

Show Illustration #13

Suddenly Boaz spotted the man. "Will you please come here?" he called. "I would like to talk to you about a business matter."

The relative came and sat with Boaz at the gate. Boaz called to ten of the most important men of Bethlehem: "Listen to what I'm going to say! I want you to witness my words."

Turning to Naomi's nearest relative, Boaz said, "You know Naomi returned recently from Moab."

"Yes, I do," he replied.

"She has a piece of land which belonged to her husband, Elimelech. She wants to sell it. I thought you should know about it because you are the closest relative. You have the right to buy it. If you do not want to purchase it, please say so. I'm the next nearest relative. If you don't want the land, I shall redeem it."

Did you know that Someone loves you and desires to redeem you? (Let students discuss. *The Lord Jesus loves you!*) In Israel, only a close relative (*a kinsman*) was able to redeem. And the only way God could redeem *us* was to send His eternal Son Jesus to earth in a human body.

2. THE NATURAL UNWORTHINESS OF RUTH
Ruth 4:5-6

Boaz's heart pounded as he waited for the relative to answer.

Speaking loudly, confidently, the closest relative replied, "I'll redeem the land." To himself he thought, *That property is valuable. I'll have it as a good inheritance for my children.*

But Boaz had more to say. "You have made a good decision. That is an excellent piece of land. But you will have another responsibility. According to God's Law, when you redeem the land you must also marry the widow, Ruth. Then she can have children who will carry on her husband's name. And *her* children will inherit the land," Boaz explained.

Show Illustration #14

"Oh, I can't marry Ruth!" the relative exclaimed. "She is a foreigner. She is a poor, unworthy widow. Whatever I have or shall buy will finally belong to my own children–not hers. No, I can't redeem Ruth." (See Deuteronomy 23:3.)

All that the relative said was true. But Boaz didn't want to redeem Ruth because she was worthy. He desired to redeem her because he *loved* her, poor as she was.

Does Ruth's unworthiness remind you of anyone you know? (Let students respond. Each should say "myself.") Listen to how God describes each of us. (Read Romans 3:10-12, 23.) Do we deserve God's love, His redemption? NO! But God loves us, unworthy as we are. Indeed, He loves us so much, He sent His Son to earth to die for us (Romans 5:8). He who had always been with God the Father became a human being so that He, the perfect One, would be related to us human beings. He is our close relative (our Kinsman). He came to earth purposely to be our Redeemer (Hebrews 2:14-15).

3. BOAZ REDEEMS RUTH
Ruth 4:7-12

Now Boaz had the right to buy from Naomi all that had belonged to her husband and sons. And best of all, he could claim Ruth as his lovely bride! According to the ancient custom of those times, to make everything legal the close relative took off his sandal and gave it to Boaz. This was a sign of agreement. The ten witnesses heard and saw all that took place.

News of what was going on at the gate quickly spread through town. Immediately a crowd gathered.

A messenger was sent to the home of Naomi where she and Ruth were waiting. "Come to the gate," he said urgently. "Bring the title for your land. Boaz is buying it."

There in the presence of the whole village, Boaz handed over the money to Naomi. Everyone listened quietly.

Show Illustration #15

Boaz announced, "You have seen that I have bought from Naomi all the property of Elimelech, Chilion, and Mahlon. I have also redeemed Ruth to be my wife. Our son will inherit this land and he will carry on the family name."

Everyone happily shouted their wishes of blessing to Boaz and Ruth.

"May you have many children!"

"May you be a great and successful man in Bethlehem!"

Ruth was happy and thankful. She was thankful he was *able to redeem her*–that he had the money needed for the purchase price. She was particularly grateful that Boaz loved her enough to redeem her.

Our Kinsman-Redeemer, the Lord Jesus Christ, had to pay a much greater price to redeem us than Boaz paid for Ruth. Listen carefully as I read. Then tell me what it cost the Lord to redeem you and me. (Read 1 Peter 1:18-19.) His blood was the purchase price for us sinners. By giving His life, He made it possible for you and me to become a part of His family.

Suppose Ruth had turned to Boaz saying, "I don't want you to redeem me." Would he have been able to redeem her? No.

She would have remained a poor, foreign widow. She never would have become a part of the Israelite family.

It is exactly the same for you and me. The Lord Jesus Christ paid the price to redeem us. His purchase sets us free from the slavery of sin and makes us a part of the family of God. But we must accept the redemption He has provided for us. Have you done this?

4. THE BLESSINGS OF REDEMPTION
Ruth 4:13-17

How do you think Ruth's life changed when she became the bride of Boaz? (Encourage student response. *She moved into his splendid home. She shared all his wealth. She no longer needed to pick up grain in his fields. She came under his protection. He provided everything she needed.*) What rich blessings she enjoyed simply because she belonged to Boaz!

Let us list some of the blessings which Christ, our Kinsman-Redeemer, provides for those who belong to Him:

1. We become a part of the family of God (John 1:12; Ephesians 2:19).
2. We share His riches (Romans 8:17; Ephesians 1:11).
3. We share His life (2 Corinthians 5:17; Galatians 2:20).
4. We shall share His heavenly home (John 14:2-3).
5. He cares for us every day (Psalm 23:1; Philippians 4:13, 19; 1 Peter 5:7).

Later, a son was born into the home of Ruth and Boaz. There was much rejoicing and thanksgiving that day. Everyone came with their best wishes.

Show Illustration #16

To Naomi they said, "How happy you must be! Now you once again have a son to carry on the name of your family." Ruth placed her treasured son in her mother-in-law's loving arms.

Yes, God has been good to me," said Naomi, her eyes sparkling. "I am thankful for Ruth. She left her homeland and her idols. She was a great help to me. Now she worships the true and living God of Heaven. And He has honored and blessed her."

As Ruth cared for the little son, I am sure she often prayed, "Dear Lord, I pray for this boy, Obed. May he love You and serve You and Your people."

God answered that prayer far above her expectations. When Obed grew to be a man, he had a son named Jesse. In time Jesse had a son named David. In manhood David became king of Israel. Generations later, from David's family the Son of God was born into the world. He was the Messiah–the One anointed by God to be the Saviour of the world.

Every Hebrew woman longed to be a mother in the line of the Messiah. This glorious privilege was given to Ruth because of God's wonderful grace.

Ruth's life began in poverty, death and mourning. It ended with happiness, new life and blessing for the whole world.

Just as God–in His grace–had a plan for Ruth, so He has a plan for your life and mine.

Will you let the Lord have His way in your life?

Will you leave the choices with Him? He is the Lord God, and He never makes mistakes.

(*Teacher:* Urge unsaved students to accept His redemption and His new life.)

www.ingramcontent.com/pod-product-compliance
Lightning Source LLC
Chambersburg PA
CBHW060802090426
42736CB00002B/127